Granny Mac A Doodle
Leave Me Be
Book One

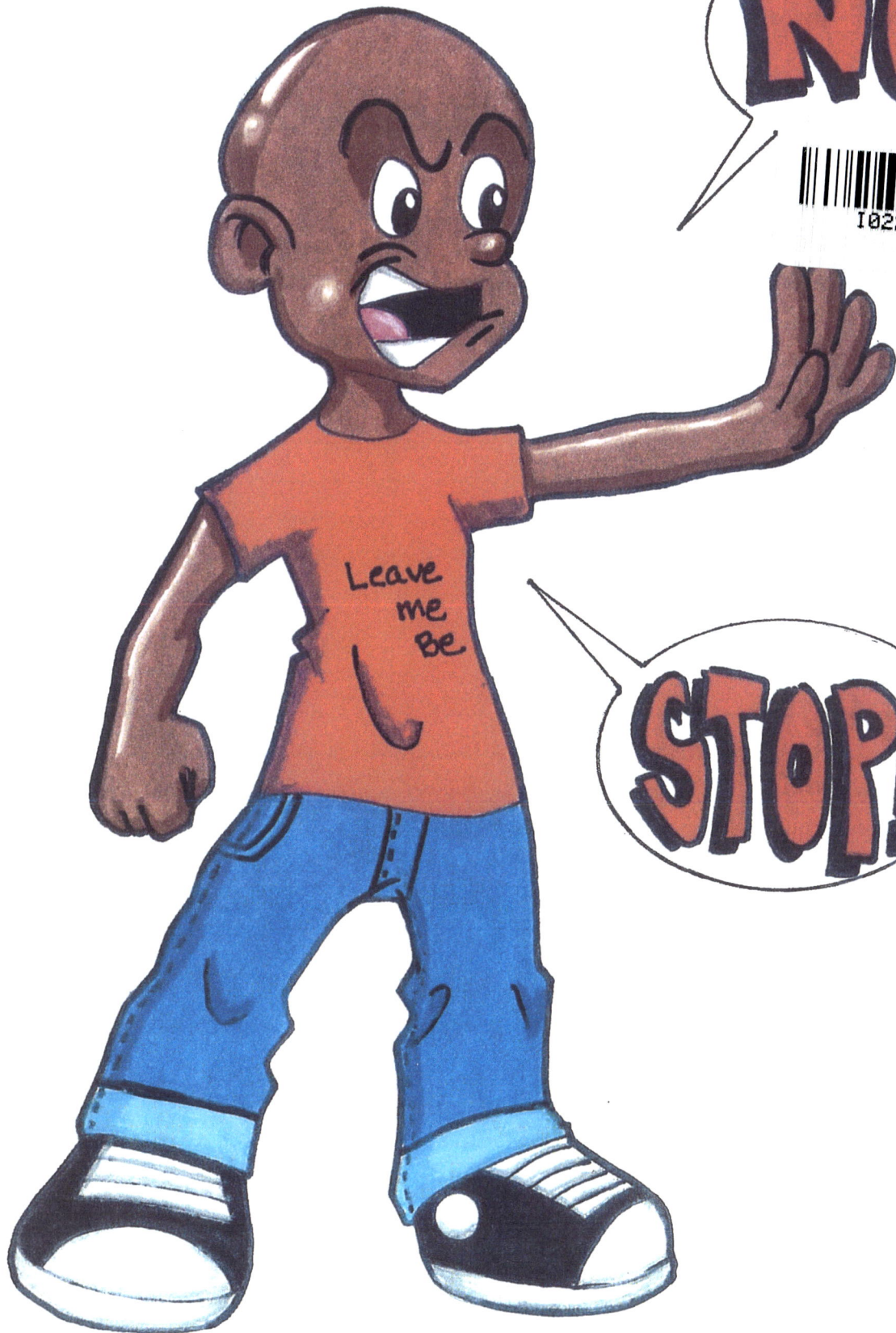

Granny Mac A Doodle
Leave Me Be
Book One

I Dedicate this book to my Grandchildren

Allannah, Amore', Arthur, C- jay, Cameron, Camile, Jalen, Jo-Jo, Kianna, Lashun, Michael, Mya, Serenity, my unborn boy and girl plus all my young friends.

Granny Mac A Doodle Leave Me Be
Book One

Notice

This book is intended as a guide to help empower young ones with knowledge and awareness. No way is it a complete antidote for all surroundings and situations. Always remember that children feel safe and protected when they have knowledge to say No, Run, and Stand firm.
This information is designed to help Parents and your young one to make informed choices. Train your young ones.

Go to: kidsandstrangers.com for more information.

Run away, yell, scream, or appeal to a nearby adult when in danger.

----- Talk to your child about what can happen----

---What If ?

What If?

---------------------You have powers that God gave you.
You can run and scream.
Scream means to utter a loud, sharp, piercing cry.
Let's try that now
together_____

_____

_____

_____

_____

_____

_____

_____

_____Rehearse often.
Children learn through Play.

What If?

_____
_____
_____
_____
_____
_____
_____
_____
_____
_____
_____
_____

Password

Mon.	Tue.	Wed.	Thurs.	Fri.

Address_____

Phone
Number_____

Father Job_____

Mother
Job_____

Pa
Cell#_____

Ma Cell #_____

What If?

----------------Are you scare, or afraid Or?

--- Would you like for
me? ---

--I love you.   You are great. Parents have you Hug
your child today?

Bullying IS a "Form of abuse" Anyone who treats other peoples especially those who are an easy target
In a cruel way is a bully. It can take the form of a Physical, Verbal, Threats, and Control.

What if? --

How?

What can we do to avoid a bully?

----------------- - _-

Teach your child to be firm and resolute if he or she is ever faced with a

With Whom?---

Why? ---

--What will happen?---

-- **Answer Every Question.**

Good Friends are fun to be with. They also can be helpful if you are

_____

_____

_____

_____

_____

_____

_____

_____

_____

_____

_____

_____

Never be by yourself when walking to school or to the library. Or?

_____

_____

_____

_____

_____

_____

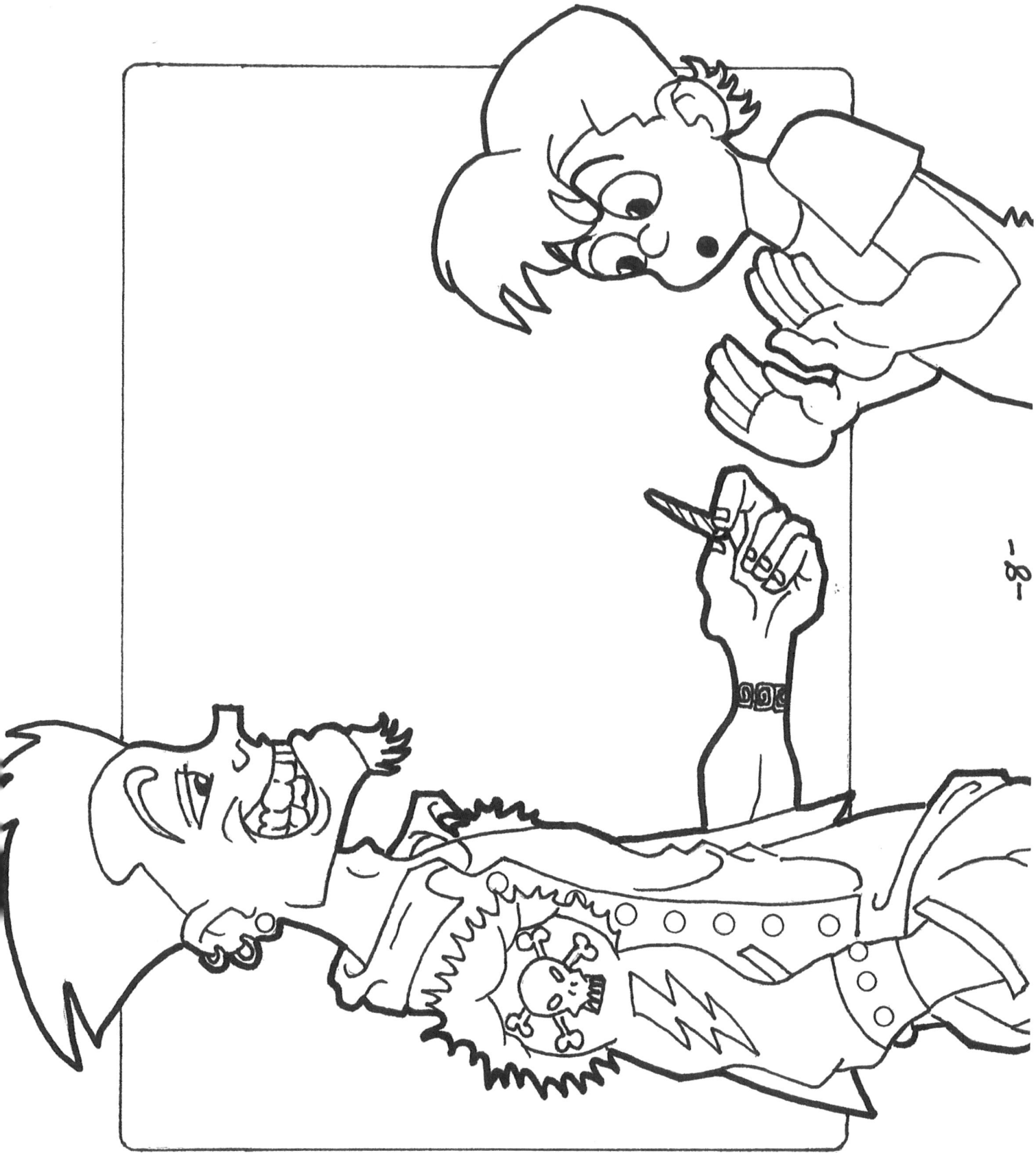

Definition for Marijuana– a preparation made from the dried flower clusters and leaves of the cannabis plant. Usually smoked or eaten.

These are some of the slang I heard when I grew up in the City- Marijuana slang: black gold, blunt, bob – Joint, pot, reefer, weed, maryjane, bammy and doobie...These are just a few. (For more Information on this timely subject, go to Marijuana Dictionary.com)

Definition for Cigarette –Tobacco (smoking substance) small roll of tobacco
Slang- butt, fag, puff, reefer, ciggy and smoke

What if---**What about Peer pressure?**---**Say NO and remove yourself from the situation.**--**Don't be afraid people are going to like if you smoke or don't smoke/ they will also like if you** -- **Have fun with this one.**

The Internet is great but?

What If? --

----------------**What will you do?**-------------------------------

----

Parents will you sit with your child?--------------------

Time

Monday	Tuesday	Wednesday	Thursday	Friday	Saturday	Sunday

------------I love you.

Listen to your children. Leave me be is for the empowerment of all children.

_____
_____
_____
_____
_____
_____
_____
_____
_____
_____
_____
_____
_____
_____
_____
_____

_____Be careful this a delicate moment in your child's
life._____
_____
_____
_____
_____
_____
_____

_____-_- Always show affection toward your child.

When training our children be at whatever level to help them. Heart to heart talks don't happen by accident.

As children grow up, it is vital for parents to help them develop their own defenses. On what do those defenses depend?

Deuteronomy 6: 6,7 And these words that I am commanding you today must prove to be on your heart; [7] and you must inculcate them in your son and speak of them when you sit in your house and when you walk on the road and when you lie down and when you get up.

1 John 4: 8 God is Love.

Showing love at a time of need is very important to a child. This will challenge you as a parent but you do have special skills.

YOUR SKILLS

1. Listen. When your child opens up to you, Please do not say things like (I will kill who ever did this) something to that affect. You will scare the child. Plus your child/children will think that you might go to jail if you did.
2. Hugs!
3. Hold your child hands.
4. Sing to your child. They may put their hands over their ears but do it anyway. (Make them laugh)
5. Take your children/child out and Bond with them.
6. Let them say crazy stuff and don't get upset.

Or you might say something positive

_____
_____
_____
_____ _ _

ANY ONE ?

Teach your child to be firm and resolute if he or she is ever faced with a molester.

With Whom?--

Why? --

--What will happen?--

-- **Answer Every Question.**

www.ingramcontent.com/pod-product-compliance
Lightning Source LLC
Chambersburg PA
CBHW042020080426
42735CB00002B/114